# Grandma

*"A loving heart is the truest wisdom."*
♡ CHARLES DICKENS

For _____

From _____

# The story of your life...

Your date and place of birth:

_____

_____

_____

Who named you, and how was your name chosen?

_____

_____

_____

_____

_____

_____

_____

Your parents' names, birthdates, and places of birth:

_____

_____

_____

_____

_____

_____

_____

_____

_____

Your brothers and sisters, oldest to youngest:

_____

_____

_____

_____

_____

_____

Your aunts and uncles:

_____

_____

_____

_____

_____

_____

Who were you closest with in your family?

_____

_____

_____

_____

_____

_____

_____

_____

Do you know anything about the history of our family?  How did we come to
this country? Where did we settle? How did we get to where we are now?

_____

_____

_____

_____

_____

_____

_____

_____

_____

_____

_____

_____

_____

_____

_____

_____

_____

_____

_____

_____

_____

_____  FAMILY

# Childhood...

What's your first memory?

_____

_____

_____

_____

_____

_____

_____

_____

_____

_____

_____

_____

_____

_____

_____

_____

_____

_____

_____

🌱 Memories... the food of our childhood, food that meant love ♥.

What kind of child were you?

What is a special memory you have of your mother?

_____

_____

_____

_____

_____

_____

_____

_____

_____

Mom

Tell me about your dad.

_____
_____
_____
_____
_____
_____
_____
_____
_____
_____
_____
_____
_____
_____
_____
_____

DaD

Tell me what you remember about your grandparents.

What were your favorite childhood pastimes?

_____
_____
_____
_____
_____
_____
_____
_____
_____

Did you play games with your family? If so, what were your favorites?

_____
_____
_____
_____
_____
_____
_____
_____
_____
_____
_____

THE BEST!

Who was the clown of your family?

_____
_____
_____
_____
_____
_____
_____
_____
_____
_____

What made you laugh?

_____
_____
_____
_____
_____
_____
_____

Family
Fun

Did you have pets?

_____

_____

_____

_____

_____

_____

_____

Describe your bedroom. Did you share your room or have it all to yourself?

_____

_____

_____

_____

_____

_____

_____

_____

_____

_____

_____

Did you have a television? What shows did you like to watch?

What was your favorite thing to eat?

_____

_____

_____

_____

_____

_____

_____

What was a special meal your mom or dad made for you?

_____

_____

_____

_____

_____

_____

_____

_____

_____

_____

_____

_____

_____

Tell me about a memorable party or celebration.

Did you help out around the house?

_____

_____

_____

_____

_____

_____

_____

_____

_____

Did you get an allowance?

_____

_____

_____

_____

_____

_____

_____

_____

_____

_____

_____

_____

_____

Who were your childhood friends?

_____
_____
_____
_____
_____
_____
_____
_____

Where did they live?

_____
_____
_____
_____
_____
_____
_____
_____
_____
_____

What was your neighborhood like?

What games did you play when you were little?

Describe a special toy. Who gave it to you? What made it so special?

Me!

What were your favorite books?

What was your favorite kind of music? How did you listen to it?

What kinds of movies did you like? Who were your favorite movie stars?
Are there any movies from that time that you still love to this day?

_____

_____

_____

_____

_____

_____

_____

_____

_____

_____

_____

_____

_____

_____

_____

_____

_____

_____

Where did you go to school?

_____

_____

_____

_____

How did you get there?

_____

_____

_____

_____

_____

_____

_____

_____

_____

_____

_____

_____

_____

_____

_____

_____

There's a back-to-school feeling in the air...

Did you like school? Did you participate in any special school events?

_____

_____

_____

_____

_____

_____

_____

_____

_____

_____

_____

School days

Which were your best subjects?

_____

_____

_____

_____

_____

_____

_____

Tell me about a special teacher you still remember.

_____

_____

_____

_____

_____

_____

_____

_____

_____

What did you typically do after school?

What were the rules of the house? Curfews?

I WANT A HOUSE THAT HAS GOT OVER ALL ITS TROUBLES; I DON'T WANT TO SPEND THE REST OF MY LIFE BRINGING UP A YOUNG & INEXPERIENCED HOUSE. ♥ JEROME K. JEROME

Are there any dreams from your childhood that you still remember?

_____

_____

_____

_____

_____

_____

_____

_____

_____

_____

_____

_____

_____

_____

_____

_____

_____

_____

_____

_____

HEARTS CAN
INSPIRE
OTHER HEARTS
WITH THEIR
FIRE. ♥

What did you do during your summers?

Did your family take trips together?

_____

_____

_____

_____

_____

_____

_____

_____

_____

_____

_____

_____

_____

_____

_____

_____

_____

_____

_____

ARE WE THERE YET?

Tell me about your religious upbringing. What were some memorable events?

_____

_____

_____

_____

_____

_____

_____

_____

_____

_____

_____

_____

_____

_____

_____

_____

_____

_____

_____

_____

_____

_____

How did your family spend the holidays?

_____

_____

_____

_____

_____

_____

_____

_____

_____

_____

_____

_____

_____

_____

_____

_____

_____

_____

_____

_____

Heirlooms we don't have in our family, but stories we've got.
— Rose Chernin

What were your favorite holiday foods?

_____

_____

_____

_____

_____

_____

_____

_____

_____

_____

_____

_____

_____

_____

_____

_____

_____

_____

_____

. . . AND IN THE WINTER, WILD & COLD, 'TIS MERRY, MERRY TOO.

Will you share a favorite holiday recipe here?

Recipe for: _____

Serves: _____

THE BEST "AROMATHERAPY" COMES  DIRECTLY FROM THE KITCHEN. ♥

Tell me a story about a holiday family gathering.

COUNTING OUR BLESSINGS

# Growing up...

What did you dream about while growing up?

_____

_____

_____

_____

_____

_____

_____

_____

_____

_____

_____

_____

_____

_____

_____

_____

_____

_____

_____

_____

_____

What did you think you would be when you grew up?

_____

_____

_____

_____

_____

_____

_____

_____

_____

_____

_____

_____

_____

AIN'T LIFE GRAND?

Did you wear makeup? Or nail polish?

_____

_____

_____

_____

_____

_____

_____

Tickle-Me Pink

How did you fix your hair?

_____

_____

_____

_____

_____

_____

_____

_____

_____

_____

_____

_____

_____

_____

_____

Describe a favorite outfit.

me
again...

Did you like fashion magazines? What did you read for fun?

_____

_____

_____

_____

_____

_____

_____

_____

_____

_____

_____

_____

_____

_____

_____

_____

_____

_____

_____

_____

_____

_____    *"All that mankind has done, thought or been:
it is in magic preservation, in the pages of books."*
❤ THOMAS CARLYLE    _____

What did you do for fun?

_____
_____
_____
_____
_____
_____
_____
_____
_____
_____
_____
_____
_____
_____
_____
_____
_____
_____

Who was your very best friend? What made you so close?

_____

_____

_____

_____

_____

_____

_____

_____

Where'd you go, what'd you do, and who'd you see together?

_____

_____

_____

_____

_____

_____

_____

_____

_____

_____

_____

_____

# FOREVER♡FRIENDS

Tell me about a best friend adventure.

_____
_____
_____
_____
_____
_____
_____
_____
_____
_____
_____
_____

Did you ever leave school with your friends without your parents' permission?

FRIENDS

If you did something that your parents didn't like, what were the consequences?

_____

_____

_____

_____

_____

_____

_____

_____

What did you do that flew under the radar?

_____

_____

_____

_____

_____

_____

_____

_____

_____

_____

_____

_____

_____

_____

Tell me about your first date: the who-what-where-when-and-why,
all the basics. How old were you? Where did you go, and what did you wear?
What did your parents have to say about all of this?

LOVE

♥ ♥ ♥

"*Love is friendship set to music.*"
Anonymous ♥

What was the biggest thing you remember happening in our country when you were in high school?

_____

_____

_____

_____

_____

_____

_____

_____

Did you pay attention to politics? What did you believe in then?

_____

_____

_____

_____

_____

_____

_____

_____

_____

_____

_____

What's the best thing that's been invented since you were younger?

_____

_____

_____

_____

_____

_____

_____

_____

_____

_____

_____

_____

_____

_____

_____

_____

_____

_____

_____

_____

_____

_____

How old were you when you got your driver's license?
Who taught you how to drive?

_____

_____

_____

_____

_____

_____

_____

_____

Tell me a story about learning to drive.

_____

_____

_____

_____

_____

_____

_____

_____

_____

_____

_____

_____

Did you go on any road trips? Share a story about a teenage adventure.

A JOY SHARED IS A JOY DOUBLED

# All grown up...

What did you do after high school? Did you go to college?

_____

_____

_____

_____

_____

_____

_____

_____

_____

OLDER
Me!

What was your first place like? Did you live alone?

HOME
SWEET
HOME

Did you like being on your own?

_____

_____

_____

_____

_____

_____

_____

_____

What did you miss about living with your parents?

_____

_____

_____

_____

_____

_____

_____

_____

_____

_____

_____

_____

Did you cook? What did you make?

Were there any restaurants you frequented? Describe the atmosphere.

What was your first job? How did you get it? Was it what you wanted to be doing?

_____

_____

_____

_____

_____

_____

_____

_____

_____

_____

_____

_____

_____

_____

_____

_____

_____

_____

_____

_____

_____

_____

What was your worst job ever? How long did you work there?

_____
_____
_____
_____
_____
_____
_____
_____
_____

If you could go back in time, what would you change about it?

_____
_____
_____
_____
_____
_____
_____
_____
_____
_____
_____
_____
_____

Write a page or two about the loves of your life.

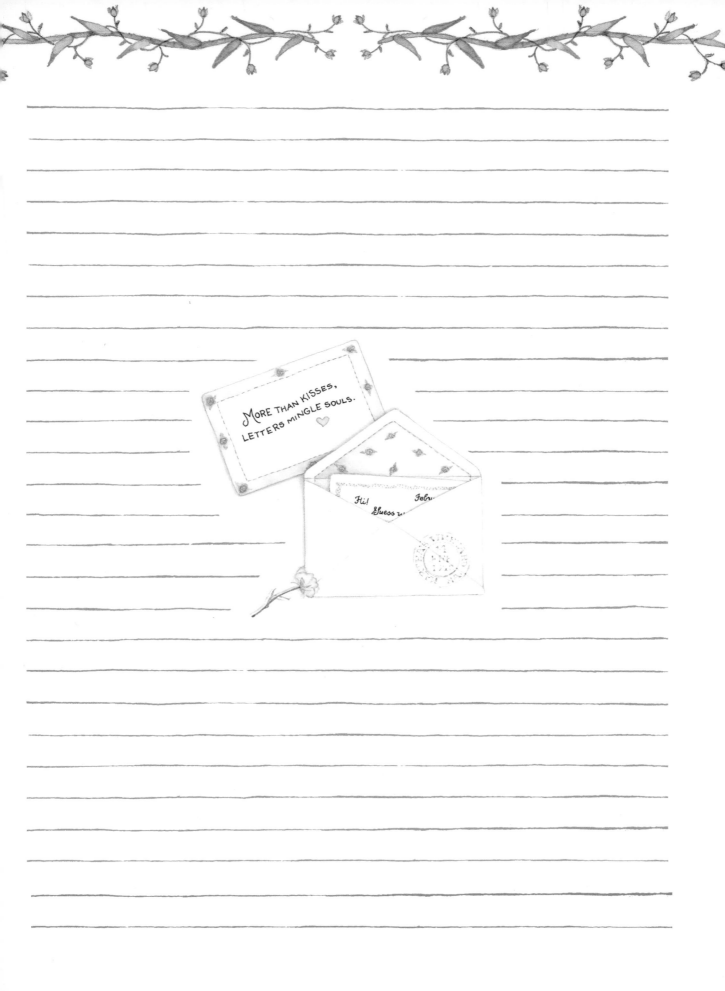

With all your expertise, can you give your best advice about relationships?

The love in your heart
wasn't put there to stay,
love isn't love
till it's
given
away.

Was there one who got away?

Did you ever fall in love at first sight?

_____

_____

_____

_____

_____

_____

_____

_____

_____

_____

_____

_____

_____

_____

_____

_____

_____

_____

_____

_____

♥ ♥ ♥ _____
_____

What was the most romantic date you ever went on?

MR. WONDERFUL

Write about my grandfather and how you met him.
How has your relationship changed over the years?

Tell me about your first home together and having your first baby.
What year was that?

_____

_____

_____

_____

_____

_____

_____

_____

_____

_____

_____

_____

BABY ANNOUNCEMENT

_____

_____

_____

_____

_____

_____

Did you enjoy being a mom?

What was your favorite thing?

What was my dad/mom like as a baby?

_____

_____

_____

_____

_____

_____

_____

_____

_____

_____

_____

_____

_____

_____

_____

_____

_____

_____

_____

_____

_____

Tell a funny story about my parent as a child.

_____

_____

_____

_____

_____

_____

_____

_____

_____

_____

_____

_____

_____

_____

_____

_____

_____

_____

_____

IF YOU DON'T WANT YOUR CHILDREN TO HEAR WHAT YOU'RE SAYING, PRETEND YOU'RE TALKING TO THEM. ♥ ANON.

Did you also work outside of the house? (How did you find the time!?)

What kinds of hobbies, activities, and vacations did you enjoy as a grown-up?

_____

_____

_____

_____

_____

_____

_____

_____

_____

_____

_____

_____

_____

_____

_____

_____

_____

_____

Where have you traveled that you loved best?

How did you spend your holidays when you had younger children?

_____
_____
_____
_____
_____
_____
_____
_____
_____

What are your favorite family traditions?

_____
_____
_____
_____
_____
_____
_____
_____
_____
_____
_____
_____

FAMILY TRADITIONS ARE THE GLUE of THE GENERATIONS.

When you heard you were going to be a grandma, how did you feel?

How old were you when I was born?

_____

_____

_____

_____

_____

_____

_____

_____

_____

_____

_____

_____

_____

_____

_____

_____

_____

_____

_____

_____

Did you babysit for me?

What did we like to do, just the two of us?

_____
_____
_____
_____
_____
_____
_____
_____
_____
_____
_____
_____
_____
_____
_____
_____
_____
_____
_____
_____

A HOUSE NEEDS A GRANDMA IN IT. ♡ Louisa May Alcott

What are the differences between your children and grandchildren?

_____
_____
_____
_____
_____
_____
_____
_____
_____

How are they similar?

_____
_____
_____
_____
_____
_____
_____
_____
_____
_____
_____
_____
_____

How has being a grandma been different than being a mom?

_____

_____

_____

_____

_____

_____

_____

_____

_____

How has it been similar?

_____

_____

_____

_____

_____

_____

_____

_____

_____

_____

_____

_____

Nobody can do for little children what grandmas do.
Grandmas sprinkle STARDUST over lives of little children.

# All about you...

What is the most surprising gift you have ever received?

_____

_____

_____

_____

_____

_____

_____

_____

_____

_____

_____

_____

_____

_____

_____

_____

_____

_____

What's your secret food addiction?

What is a favorite family recipe of yours? Why is it special?

_____

_____

_____

_____

_____

_____

_____

_____

_____

_____

_____

_____

_____

_____

_____

_____

_____

_____

_____

Will you write it down here?

Recipe for: _____

Serves: _____

_____

_____

_____

_____

_____

_____

_____  *Love*

_____

_____

_____

_____

_____

_____

_____

_____

_____

SO GOOD ♥

What's your favorite quote, and why?

_____

_____

_____

_____

_____

_____

_____

_____

What's a favorite piece of jewelry that you own?

_____

_____

_____

_____

_____

_____

_____

_____

_____

_____

_____

_____

Who are your heroes?

What do you love to do?

If you could be any age, which would you choose?

_____

_____

_____

_____

_____

_____

_____

_____

_____

_____

_____

_____

_____

_____

_____

_____

_____

_____

_____

"Backward, turn backward, O Time in your flight;
Make me a child again just for tonight." ♥

Elizabeth Akers Allen

If you could do it all over again, would you change anything?

_____

_____

_____

_____

_____

_____

_____

_____

_____

_____

_____

_____

_____

_____

_____

_____

_____

_____

_____

_____

_____

_____

What hopes and dreams do you have for the future?

What would you most like to be remembered for?

_____

_____

_____

_____

_____

_____

_____

_____

_____

_____

_____

_____

_____

_____

_____

_____

_____

_____

" There's absolutely no reason for being rushed along with the rush. Everybody should be free to go very slow."

Robt. Frost

What is your best advice about life?

_____

_____

_____

_____

_____

_____

_____

_____

_____

_____

_____

_____

_____

_____

_____

_____

_____

_____

_____

_____

THE BEST THINGS IN
LIFE AREN'T THINGS. ♡

What makes you the happiest?

A picture is worth a thousand words.

What is the most important thing you have learned?

_____

_____

_____

_____

_____

_____

_____

_____

_____

_____

_____

_____

_____

_____

_____

_____

_____

_____

_____

_____

Hours fly
Flowers die
New days
New ways
Pass by
Love stays ♥

A loving heart is the truest wisdom.
♥ CHARLES DICKENS

# More stories...

Picture Perfect

# memories

WHERE SHALL I
BEGIN? WHICH
OF MY IMPORTANT
THINGS SHALL I
TELL YOU FIRST?
Jane Austen

# Special Times

There are only two ways to live your life. One is as though nothing is a miracle. The other is as if everything is.
ALBERT EINSTEIN

# Precious Moments

A picture goes here;
your family, your house,
your dog, your cat —
but best would be
YOU
since this is your book. ♥

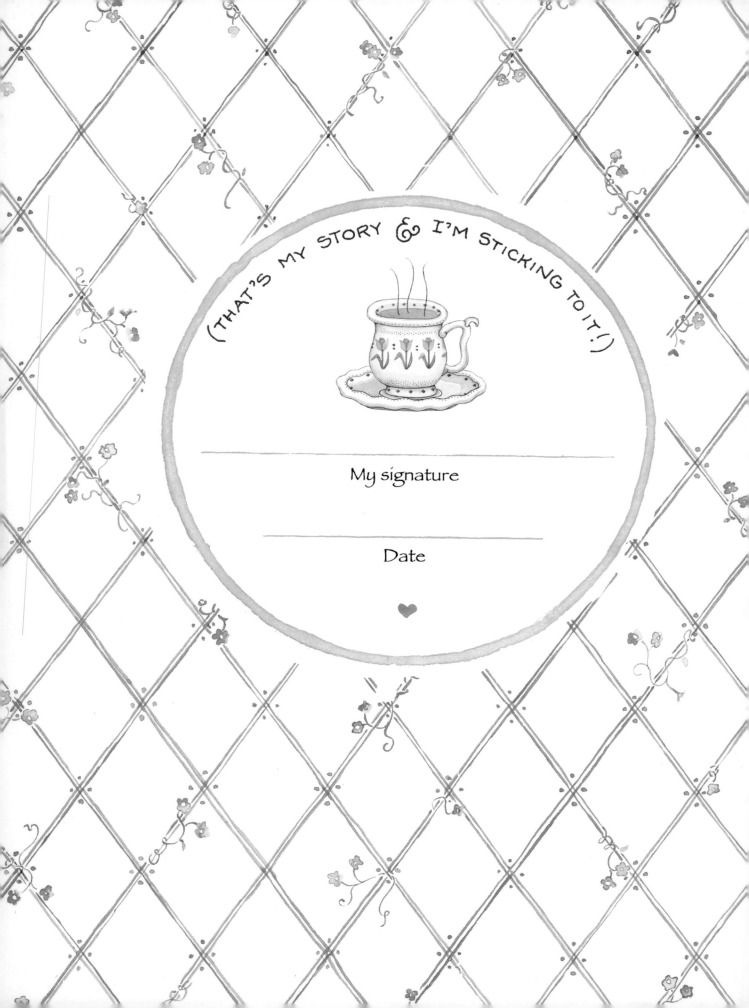

(THAT'S MY STORY & I'M STICKING TO IT!)

_____

My signature

_____

Date

♥